The Ultimate Survival Guide

James R. Tolliver

ISBN-13: 978-1482361629

ISBN-10: 1482361620

SPECIAL THANKS TO

FIELD EXPERT

TD BENTLEY

SURVIVAL FOODS CONSULTANT

PHYLLIS SLONE

OTHER SURVIVAL TIPS

Information courtesy of the U.S. Army Survival Manual

Research and examples from various non copyright internet materials.

CONTENTS

This is a survival manual has been put together to help aid in the survival of a total society collapse, terrorist attack, or an invading force who would pose a threat and individuals would be forced to survive when there is the following conditions;

There is no one to call for help

When survival while barricaded in their homes would be necessary

When they may have to leave their homes and survive in the open elements

When food may not be readily available

When they may be required to live off the land

hen water may be contaminated and may have to know

How to filter and purify water that is available to survive

When self protection may be all the protection that exist

Well let's start with the basics. **In the event of a disaster, nuclear attack, or an over throw of our government, would you know how to survive?**

The communications are down, our infrastructure has been destroyed, help is not coming, only the strong will survive, what will you do?

This guide is not only a how to survive, but how to prepare before an event occurs. Preparation meets opportunity equals success is what a wise man once told me. Without preparation your chances of survival is very minimal at best. Preparation is your only hope in a catastrophic event, in a total melt down of the government or a nuclear war.

This guide will show you some things that can be done before and during an apocalypse type situation.

- *What can you do to prepare?*

- *What items should be ready before hand?*

- *Where should you go?*

- *How can you build shelter?*

- *How do you build a fire?*

- *What foods can be eaten in the wild?*

- *What if you get sick?*

These are a few things that will help you survive, eat, stay warm, and protect yourself in the event of something that would send the population into a dog eat dog scenario.

Being ready before hand is key.

Mentally can you be ready, the answer is yes. If you have prepared before this event occurs, you will not be the one running around trying to figure out what to do.

Physically are you ready, this is part of being prepared. Having a regular workout schedule will be the key for the physical demands that will be required to survive in harsh conditions. Everyone has a different physical activity level that they can achieve so try to step it up your physical condition a few notches. Would you be able to walks miles a day, can you lift 75 pounds or more, can you defend yourself in hand to hand combat if need be.

Having an ample supply of emergency supplies around the home if a disaster or a catastrophic event occurred. Generator, fuel, flashlights, oil lamps, candles, food, water, water purification, short wave radio, first aid supplies, daily medication, a way to stay warm, a way to defend yourself and your family etc. What about a shelter? Basements, cellars, any way to get out of harm's way may be vital in staying alive in the event of a NBC (Nuclear Biological or Chemical) attack.

What if you had to leave your home? Having the basic survival supplies to be able to take with you in the event that you would need to leave your home may mean the difference between life and death.

Planning and Preparation

Now that I have scared you and showed you what could occur. What should you do to be prepared? Let's start with Some common sense tips. If you have a family, have an Emergency preparedness plan.

Where would you meet in an emergency and no communication would be possible. Pick a place everyone could get to quickly. Have what has been called an action packer. Totes with emergency supplies that can be grabbed in a hurry.

Now where will you go? Do you have a plan of possible places that you could go. A secluded farm, cabin in the hills, forest or hilly area with areas suitable for shelter, food, fresh water, places to take cover if an invading army were present or a total society melt down were to occur.

Once you and your family makes it to your destination, its time to set up camp in an area that easily defended higher up where you can see far off, or in a cellar, cave, or some area that you will not be found.

If no shelter is present then gathering materials to make a shelter will be priority number one. Later in this book there are instructions for building shelter suitable for survival.

Once shelter has been constructed, then making sure that everyone stays warm is the second priority. Exposure in the open elements will be your worst enemy. There will be no one to call for help. No ambulance, no hospital, no doctor, you must be careful because now a simple cold or cut can kill you.

Gather food and setting traps will be your next priority. Eating will now be a survival task. The days of enjoying food and being able to pick and choose what you like to eat has now been transformed to obtaining high protein and high calorie foods to stay alive. Sure you have packed food, but that is not going to be enough to keep you alive for very long. Hunting and gathering will be how you may have to survive until society returns to normal if at all.

As you go through the rest of the manual, you will learn the basic survival skills needed to survive. It would be a good idea to practice what you learn in this book and to purchase other books or manuals to have in your action packers for reference. You have to keep in mind is that there is not going to be any help, no one to call, no internet to look up information to find out how to do something. This book and any other books will be your only reference. Read it, practice making fires, learn what plants you can and can't eat, your life depends on it.

It is my hope that all this information will be kept and never used. But in the events described as "Dooms Day", "Apocalypse", "NBC (Nuclear Biological or Chemical) Attack", this book may be all the information that you have.

Being prepared to survive means the following;

You must be ready mentally

You must have the knowledge within this book

You must be physically capable

You must have a emergency plan of action

You must have supplies to get you started

You must be ready to take action in a matter of minuets

SURVIVAL KITS

The environment is the key to the types of items you will need in your survival kit. How much equipment you put in your kit depends on how you will carry the kit. A kit carried on your body will have to be smaller than one carried in a vehicle. Always layer your survival kit, keeping the most important items on your body. For example, your map and compass should always be on your body. Carry less important items on your load-bearing equipment. Place bulky items in the rucksack.

In preparing your survival kit, select items you can use for more than one purpose. If you have two items that will serve the same function, pick the one you can use for another function. Do not duplicate items, as this increases your kit's size and weight.

Your survival kit need not be elaborate. You need only functional items that will meet your needs and a case to hold the items. For the case, you might want to use a Band-Aid box, a first aid case, an ammunition pouch, or another suitable case. This case should be--

- Water repellent or waterproof.
- Easy to carry or attach to your body.
- In your survival kit, you should have--
- Water purification tablets or drops.
- Fire starting equipment.
- Signaling items.
- Food procurement items.
- Shelter items.
- Some examples of these items are--
- Lighter, metal match, waterproof matches.
- Snare wire.
- Signaling mirror.
- Wrist compass.

- Fish and snare line.
- Fishhooks.
- Candle.
- Small hand lens.
- Ox tetracycline tablets (diarrhea or infection).
- Water purification tablets.
- Solar blanket.
- Surgical blades.
- Butterfly sutures.
- Condoms for water storage.
- Chap Stick.
- Needle and thread.
- Knife.

Selecting the appropriate wilderness survival gear is important to have a safe wilderness trip. However, remember your most important survival gear is your brain! Mental preparedness, knowledge and skills are a must, without that, nothing else really matters.

Backpacking gear

This is a necessity to be able to transport basic survival gear, food, and weapons.

Medium Size AX and Shovel

These will come in handy as you build shelter and sometimes prepare food.

Lighters and matches is good for emergencies, but building a fire with alternative methods should be used to conserved because you may not know how long you may be out there before you can replenish these items.

First aid kit

These are one of the things that will get used the most in your first aid kit, especially if you have kids. You will want to make sure you have plenty of them and that you have a variety of shapes and sizes. Regular size bandages will suffice for most things, but having a few larger ones is wise. The small ones are perfect for tiny cuts on young children.

Other Types of Bandages
Gauze bandages are helpful for large scrapes or burns. The 4 x 4 sterile gauze bandages are also great for cleaning cuts and scrapes. You will want to keep medical adhesive tape on hand as well for taping down the gauze. You can also buy very large bandages that do not need tape. An Ace bandage is a handy item to have on hand for minor sprains.

Medicines
Your first aid kit is not the place to store prescription medications, but you will want to have some simple over-the-counter items available. Anesthetic sprays or lotions provide relief from sunburn, insect bites and rashes. Antibiotic cream prevents infections in minor open wounds and is a must in your kit. Cough medicine, aspirin, ibuprofen and anti-diarrhea medicines are helpful during cold and flu season. Other helpful medications are charcoal, in case of accidental poisoning, and children's versions of over-the-counter medicines.

Other Necessary Items

Other items you will want to have in your first aid kit include:

- Small scissors, for cutting bandages and clothing
- Tweezers, for removing splinters
- Thermometer
- Insect repellant
- Plastic gloves-always wear these when treating open wounds
- Antiseptic wipes, great for cleaning minor cuts and scrapes
- Toothache medication
- Sandwich bags that seal-these are great for ice packs. Just throw in some ice cubes and you have some instant ice packs.

Weapons and Ammunitions

Because you may not know who you may encounter and if you will be able to get help, be prepared to defend yourself.

1. Hand to hand combat is reliable and can be used without alarming other persons who may mean you harm.
2. Walking stick is universal and is usually handy for quick access. It is also another weapon that can be used quietly and doesn't draw attention.
3. Survival knife although lethal but is very effective and universal and it is also another weapon that can be used quietly and doesn't draw attention.
4. Hand gun is very effective easy to carry and is best for self defense.
5. Rifle or shot gun is the weapon of choice because of being universal in self defense and for hunting food.

Surviving A Nuclear Attack

Be prepared, supplies ready and ready to handle the what if scenario's.

Note

Stay Informed, watch the news. Most likely there will be plenty of warning prior to a nuclear attack if from another county. Watch the news, you will know the countries with nuclear capabilities and the unrest that will occur prior to the attack. A nuclear attack will unlikely be a surprise from an enemy nation. Such an attack would likely be preceded by a deteriorating political situation. A war with conventional weapons between nations that both have nuclear weapons, if not ended swiftly, may escalate towards nuclear war; and even limited nuclear strikes in one region carry the likelihood to escalate towards an all-out nuclear war elsewhere.

Days and hours prior to the attack being prepared to evacuation if a nuclear exchange is looking likely. If evacuation is not an option, then it should at least affect the kind of shelter you will construct for yourself. Learn your proximity to the following targets and plan appropriately:

Military bases, government facilities, and especially those known to house nuclear bombers, ballistic missile submarines, or ICBM silos. These are certain to be attacked even in a limited nuclear exchange.

Major ports and runways over 10,000 feet long. These are likely to be attacked even in a limited nuclear exchange, and certain to be attacked in an all-out nuclear war.

Centers of large cities. These are likely to be attacked even in a limited nuclear exchange and certain to be attacked in an all-out nuclear war.

Industrial cities and major population centers. These are likely to be attacked in the event of an all-out nuclear war. Learn about the different types of nuclear weapons.:

Fission (A-Bombs) are the most basic nuclear weapon and are incorporated into the other weapon classes. This bomb's power comes from splitting heavy nuclei (plutonium and uranium) with neutrons; as the uranium or plutonium split each atom releases great amounts of energy - *and more neutrons*. The *daughter neutrons* cause an extremely fast nuclear chain reaction. Fission bombs are the only type of nuclear bomb used in war so far.

Fusion (H-Bombs), using the incredible heat of a fission bomb 'spark plug', compress and heat deuterium and tritium (isotopes of hydrogen) which fuse, releasing immense amounts of energy. Fusion weapons are also known as thermonuclear weapons since high temperatures are required to fuse deuterium and tritium; such weapons are usually *many* times more powerful than the bombs that destroyed Nagasaki and Hiroshima.

Protect critical electrical equipment against EMP. A nuclear weapon detonated at a very high altitude will generate an electromagnetic pulse so powerful that it can destroy electronic and electrical devices. At the very least, unplug all devices from electrical sockets and antennas. Placing radios, flashlights in a sealed metal container (a "Faraday cage") may protect from EMP, providing the items being protected are *not* in contact with the enclosure. The metal shield must surround the protected item completely - and it helps if it is grounded.

The items to be protected should be insulated from the conductive shell, since the EMP field washing over the shield can still induce voltages in solid state circuit boards. A metalized space blanket wrapped securely around a device wrapped in newspaper or cotton may act as a Faraday shield, helpful if one is far from the blast.

Another way is to wrap a cardboard box in copper or aluminum foil. Place the item in there and plug the device into the ground.

Seek shelter immediately. Aside from the geopolitical warning signs, your first warnings of an imminent nuclear attack will most likely be an alarm or warning signal; if not, it will be the blast itself. The bright light from a detonation of a nuclear weapon can be seen tens of miles away from ground zero. If within the vicinity of the blast (or ground zero), your chances of survival are virtually nonexistent unless you are in a shelter that provides a very (VERY) good blast protection. If you are a few miles out, you will have about 10-15 seconds until the heat wave hits you, and maybe 20-30 seconds until the shock wave does. *Under no circumstances should you look directly at the fireball.* On a clear day, this can cause temporary blindness at very large distances. However, the actual damage radius is highly variable depending on the size of the bomb, the altitude of the explosion, and even the weather conditions at the time of the blast

If you can't find shelter, seek a depressed area nearby and lay face down, exposing as little skin as possible. If there is no shelter of this kind, dig as fast as possible. Even around 8 kilometers (5 miles) you will suffer third degree thermal-burns; still at 32 kilometers (20 miles) the heat can burn the skin off your body. The wind itself will peak at around 960 kilometers per hour (600mph) and will level anything or anybody caught in the open.

Failing the above options, get indoors, if, and only if, you can be sure that the building will not suffer significant blast and heat damage. This will, at least, provide some protection against radiation. Whether this will be a viable option depends on the construction of the building and how close you will be to the likely ground zero of a nuclear strike. Stay well away from any windows, preferably in a room without one; even if the building does not suffer substantial damage, a nuclear explosion will blow out windows at enormous distances.

Don't be surrounded by anything flammable or combustible. Substances like nylon or any oil based material will ignite from the heat.

Remember that radiation exposure could cause large numbers of deaths.

Initial (prompt) radiation. This is radiation released at the moment of detonation, and it is short-lived and travels short distances. With the large yields of modern nuclear weapons, it is thought that this will kill few who would not be killed by the blast or heat at the same distance.

Residual radiation. Known as radiation fallout. If the detonation was a surface blast or the fireball hits the earth, large amounts of fallout occurs. The dust and debris kicked into the atmosphere rains down, bringing with it dangerous amounts of radiation. The fallout may rain down as contaminated black soot known as "black rain," which is very fatal and may be of extreme temperature. Fallout will contaminate anything it touches.

Once you have survived the blast and the initial radiation (for now at least; radiation symptoms have an incubation period), you must find protection against the burning black soot.

Know the types of radiation particles. Before we continue, we should mention the three different types:

Alpha particles. These are the weakest and, during an attack, are virtually non-existent as a threat. Alpha particles will survive for only a couple inches in the air before they are absorbed by the atmosphere. They possess a minuscule threat from the exterior, however, they will be fatal if ingested or inhaled. Standard clothing will help protect you from Alpha particles.

Beta particles: These are faster than Alpha particles and can penetrate further. They will travel for up to 10 meters (10 yards) before they are absorbed into the atmosphere. Exposure to beta particles is not fatal unless exposed for prolonged periods; which may cause "Beta burns," almost like painful sunburn. They pose a serious threat, however, to the eyes, should they be exposed for a prolonged period. Once again this is harmful if ingested or inhaled, and clothing will help prevent Beta burns.

Gamma Rays. Gamma Rays are the deadliest. They can travel for nearly a mile in the air and penetrate just about any kind of shielding. Therefore gamma radiation will cause severe damage to the internal organs even as an external source. Sufficient shielding will be required.

A shelter's PF against radiation will tell you how many times less a person inside the shelter will receive radiation compared to open space. For example, RPF 300 means that you will receive 300 times less radiation in the shelter than in the open.

Avoid exposure to Gamma radiation. Try not to spend more than 5 minutes exposed. If you are in a rural area, try finding a cave, or a fallen log into which you can crawl. Otherwise just dig a trench to lie in, with stacked earth around you.

Begin reinforcing your shelter from the inside by stacking dirt around the walls or anything else you can find. If in a trench, then create a roof, but only if materials are nearby; don't expose yourself when not necessary.

Plan on staying in your shelter for a minimum of 200 hours (8-9 days). Under no circumstances leave the shelter in the first forty-eight hours .

Ration your supplies. You will need to ration to survive, obviously; therefore you will eventually expose yourself to the radiation (unless you are in a specific shelter with food and water).

Processed foods are okay to eat, so long as the container has no punctures and is relatively intact.

Animals may be eaten but, they must be skinned carefully with the heart, liver and kidneys discarded. Try not to eat meat that is close to the bone, for bone marrow retains radiation.

Plants in a "hot zone" are edible; those with edible roots or undergrowth (carrots, potatoes...) are highly recommended. Use an edibility test on the plants. See How to Test if a Plant Is Edible.

Open water may have received fallout particles and is harmful. Water from an underground source, such as a spring or covered well, is your best bet. (Consider making a basic pit-style solar still, as described in How to Make Water in the Desert.) Use water from streams and lakes only as a last resort. Create a filter by digging a hole about 1ft from the bank and drawing the water which seeps in. It may be cloudy or muddy so allow the sediments to sit, then boil the water to ensure safety from bacteria. If in a building, the water is usually safe. If there is no water (there most likely won't be), use the water already in the pipes by opening the faucet at the highest point of the house to let in air, then open a faucet at the lowest point of the house to drain the water.

Wear all clothing (hats, gloves, goggles, closed sleeve shirt, etc.), especially when outside to help prevent Beta burns. Decontaminate by shaking your clothes constantly and washing, with water, any exposed skin; settled residue will eventually cause burns.

Treat radiation and thermal burns.

Minor Burn. Also known as a Beta burn (though it may be from other particles). Immerse Beta burns in cold water until the pain subsides (usually 5 minutes).

If skin starts to blister, char or break; wash it with cold water to remove contaminants, then cover with a sterile compress to prevent infection. Do not break the blisters!

If the skin does not blister, char or break; don't cover it, even if it covers a large portion of the body (almost like sunburn). Instead, wash the area and cover it with Vaseline or a solution of baking powder and water if available. But, moist (uncontaminated) earth will do.

Severe Burn. Known as a thermal burn, as it comes mostly from the high intensity blast heat, rather than ionizing particles, though it can be from the latter. This can be life threatening; everything becomes a factor: water loss, shock, lung damage, infection, etc. Follow these steps to treat a severe burn.

Protect burns from further contamination.

If clothing covers the burn area, gently cut and remove the cloth from the burn. *DO NOT* try to remove cloth which has stuck or fused onto the burn. *DO NOT* try to pull clothes over the burn. *DO NOT* put any ointment on the burn.

Gently wash the burned area with water ONLY. Do NOT apply creams or ointments.

Do NOT use a normal sterile medical dressing not specifically intended for burns. As non-adhesive burn dressings (and all other medical supplies) are likely to be in short supply, an expedient alternative is to use plastic wrap (also known as saran wrap, food wrap, and cling film), which is sterile, does not stick to burns, and is readily available.

Prevent shock. Shock is the inadequate flow of blood to the vital tissues and organs. If untreated, it can be fatal. Shock results from excessive blood loss, deep burns, or reactions to the sight of a wound or blood. The signs are restlessness, thirst, pale skin and rapid heartbeat. Sweating may occur even if the skin feels cool and clammy. As it worsens, they breathe short fast.

Radiation Syndrome is not contagious, and everything depends on the amount of radiation one received.

Most likely, a nuclear attack will not be a singular event. Be prepared for another strike or strikes by enemy nations, or an invasion by the attacking party.

Be prepared for another blast. Keep your shelter intact, unless the materials used are absolutely necessary for survival. Collect any excess clean water and food that is available.

Treating Radiation Poisoning

If radiation poisoning is suspected treat with the following;

Potassium iodide is another common treatment option for radiation poisoning. Potassium iodine collects in the thyroid. It takes up space that radioactive iodine would occupy. Without room to stay in the thyroid, the radioactive iodine is sent out of the thyroid and excreted with urine.

Diethylenetriamine pentacetic acid, or DTPA, is another common form of treatment for radiation poisoning. Radiation poisoning can often come from exposure to the radioactive metals of americium, curium and plutonium. Upon exposure these elements can lodge in the body. DPTA binds to the metals. It is then excreted in urine or feces.

Prussian blue may also be used to treat radiation poisoning. Like DTPA, Prussian blue binds with radioactive particles in the body. However, instead of radioactive metals, Prussian blue binds with two other types of radioactive elements called thallium and cesium. When taken directly after exposure, Prussian blue is able to remove many of the radioactive particles before the cells can absorb them. Once attached to the radioactive particles, the Prussian blue exits the body in the feces, taking along the particles.

How to build a wilderness shelter

Building a survival shelter is an absolute priority, if you face a survival situation in harsh or unpredictable weather. A good shelter must protect you from the elements and be comfortable enough for resting and sleeping. Most people cannot survive unprotected from rough weather for more than a few hours.

If possible choose ground:

• that is dry, well drained and reasonably flat.

• that is a comfortable distance to water and has a supply of firewood.

• that has building materials for your shelter.

• that provides protection against strong winds.

If you are lost and people are looking for you, make sure your shelter site is easy to be seen and found by search and rescue teams.

Unsuitable shelter sites:

- A site too close to water may lead you to be troubled by insects.

- Rivers presents a constant threat to safety. Heavy rainfall in nearby hills can easily create flash floods. Avoid dry riverbeds.

- Avoid loose rocks, dead trees or other natural growth that could fall on your shelter.

- Low ground, such as ravines and narrow valleys, could be damp and collect the heavy cold air at night and are therefore be colder than the surrounding high ground. On the other hand, the tops of mountains are exposed to higher winds. The best area to seek shelter is somewhere in between.

Most Practical Shelter For Wilderness Survival

Start with the basic skeleton of the shelter

TENT AND TARP **SHELTERS**

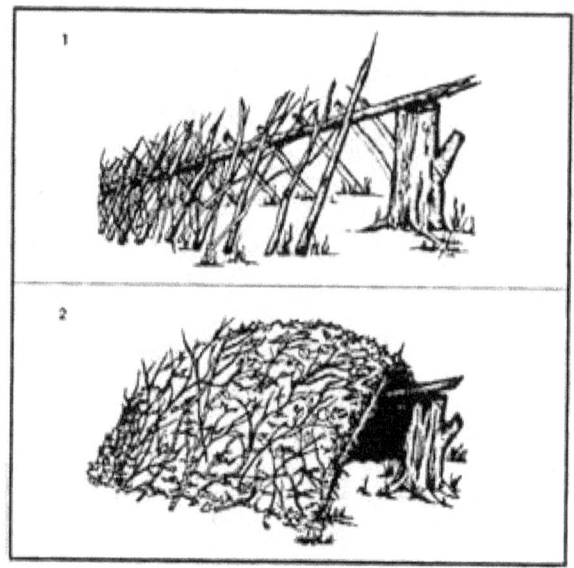

Figure 5-11. Debris hut.

After completion find light grass, weeds for insulation and for a soft place to lay.

HOW TO LIGHT A FIRE

Always light your fire from the upwind side. Make sure to lay your tinder, kindling, and fuel so that your fire will burn as long as you need it. Igniters provide the initial heat required to start the tinder burning. They fall into two categories: modern methods and primitive methods.

Modern Methods

Modem igniters use modem devices--items we normally think of to start a fire.

Matches

Make sure these matches are waterproof. Also, store them in a waterproof container along with a dependable striker pad.

Convex Lens

Use this method only on bright, sunny days. The lens can come from binoculars, camera, telescopic sights, or magnifying glasses. Angle the lens to concentrate the sun's rays on the tinder. Hold the lens over the same spot until the tinder begins to smolder. Gently blow or fan the tinder into flame, and apply it to the fire lay.

Metal Match

Place a flat, dry leaf under your tinder with a portion exposed. Place the tip of the metal match on the dry leaf, holding the metal match in one hand and a knife in the other. Scrape your knife against the metal match to produce sparks. The sparks will hit the tinder. When the tinder starts to smolder.

Battery

Use a battery to generate a spark. Use of this method depends on the type of battery available. Attach a wire to each terminal. Touch the ends of the bare wires together next to the tinder so the sparks will ignite it.

Gunpowder

Often, you will have ammunition with your equipment. If so, carefully extract the bullet from the shell casing, and use the gunpowder as tinder. A spark will ignite the powder. Be extremely careful when extracting the bullet from the case.

Primitive Methods

Primitive igniters are those attributed to our early ancestors.

Flint and Steel

The direct spark method is the easiest of the primitive methods to use. The flint and steel method is the most reliable of the direct spark methods. Strike a flint or other hard, sharp-edged rock edge with a piece of carbon steel (stainless steel will not produce a good spark). This method requires a loose-jointed wrist and practice. When a spark has caught in the tinder, blow on it. The spark will spread and burst into flames.

Fire-Plow

The fire-plow is a friction method of ignition. You rub a hardwood shaft against a softer wood base. To use this method, cut a straight groove in the base and plow the blunt tip of the shaft up and down the groove. The plowing action of the shaft pushes out small particles of wood fibers. Then, as you apply more pressure on each stroke, the friction ignites the wood particles.

Bow and Drill

The technique of starting a fire with a bow and drill is simple, but you must exert much effort and be persistent to produce a fire. You need the following items to use this method:

Socket.

The socket is an easily grasped stone or piece of hardwood or bone with a slight depression in one side. Use it to hold the drill in place and to apply downward pressure.

Drill.

The drill should be a straight, seasoned hardwood stick about 2 centimeters in diameter and 25 centimeters long. The top end is round and the low end blunt (to produce more friction).

Fire board.

Its size is up to you. A seasoned softwood board about 2.5 centimeters thick and 10 centimeters wide is preferable. Cut a depression about 2 centimeters from the edge on one side of the board. On the underside, make a V-shaped cut from the edge of the board to the depression.

Bow.

The bow is a resilient, green stick about 2.5 centimeters in diameter and a string. The type of wood is not important. The bowstring can be any type of cordage. You tie the bowstring from one end of the bow to the other, without any slack.

To use the bow and drill, first prepare the fire lay. Then place a bundle of tinder under the V-shaped cut in the fire board. Place one foot on the fire board. Loop the bowstring over the drill and place the drill in the precut depression on the fire board. Place the socket, held in one hand, on the top of the drill to hold it in position. Press down on the drill and saw the bow back and forth to twirl the drill. Once you have established a smooth motion, apply more downward pressure and work the bow faster. This action will grind hot black powder into the tinder, causing a spark to catch. Blow on the tinder until it ignites.

How to make water safe to drink

Water is one of your most urgent needs in a survival situation. You can't live long without it, especially in hot areas where you lose water rapidly through perspiration. Even in cold areas, you need a minimum of 2 liters of water each day to maintain efficiency.

More than three-fourths of your body is composed of fluids. Your body loses fluid as a result of heat, cold, stress, and exertion. To function effectively, you must replace the fluid your body loses. So, one of your first goals is to obtain an adequate supply of water

Water purification

There are three ways to treat suspected water: filtration, boiling and chemical water purification.

· Filtering water doesn't purify it, but it reduces particles and sediment and makes the water taste better.

Knowing how to make a water filter is important, if the only water you can find is dirty muddy water. There are a number of different ways to make a water filter. One simple way is to use sand. Sand is nature's way of purifying water.

Simple sand water filter

1. To start with, you need a container. If you can find a large, empty can, use it. Punch 5-10 holes in the bottom of the can. A large plastic bottle is also fine. Cut the end of the bottle off evenly. If there is no container available, you have to use what material that nature can provide, or that you brought with you.

If you find a birch tree, make a cone of birch bark. The cone will need to have a fairly small hole in the bottom. Tie the cone with rope to keep it from opening up.

2. First, you need to stop the sand to get out of the container. Find some filter material you can place at the bottom. For instance:

• a couple of inches (centimeters) of pebbles.
• a grass mesh, make sure it's nonpoisonous grass.
• or cotton material.

3. Add a layer of gravel. The main purpose of the gravel layer is to strengthen the filter material and prevent sand mixed with the water you get from the filter.

4. Fill your bottle or cone with sand.

5. Collect some water. Pour your collected water through the filter. Catch it in another container at the bottom. Look at the water that comes out of the filter. It should be clear. If not, you may have to pass the water through the filter more than once.

Safe water

Now you know how to make a water filter, but to get safe water to drink, you also have to purify your water. The water may still contain harmful bacteria that your filter did not remove.

To improve your water filter, add a layer of charcoal between the gravel and sand layer. Get charcoal from your fire, crush it, not to powder but just fine gravel size.

· Boiling is the most certain way of killing all microorganisms. However, boiling will NOT neutralize chemical pollutants.

· To purify water with chemicals, use **water purification tablets** that should be included in your survival kit.

Extreme Cold Weather Survival Tips

It is more difficult for you to satisfy your basic water, food and shelter needs in a cold environment than in a warm environment. Even if you have the basic requirements, you must also have adequate protective clothing and the will to survive. The will to survive is as important as the basic needs. There have been incidents when trained and well-equipped individuals have not survived cold weather situations because they lacked the will to live. Conversely, this will has sustained individuals less well-trained and equipped

Weather Survival

You must not only have enough clothing to protect you from the cold, you must also know how to maximize the warmth you get from it. For example, always keep your head covered. You can lose 40 percent to 45 percent of body heat from an unprotected head and even more from the unprotected neck, wrists and ankles. These areas of the body are good radiators of heat and have very little insulating fat. The brain is very susceptible to cold and can stand the least amount of cooling. Because there is much blood circulation in the head, most of which is on the surface, you can lose heat quickly if you do not cover your head.

There are four basic principles to follow to keep warm. An easy way to remember these basic principles is to use the word "COLD."

C: Keep clothing clean

This principle is always important for sanitation and comfort. In winter, it is also important from the standpoint of warmth. Clothes matted with dirt and grease lose much of their insulation value. Heat can escape more easily from the body through the clothing's crushed or filled up air pockets.

O: Avoid overheating

When you get too hot, you sweat and your clothing absorbs the moisture. This affects your warmth in two ways: dampness decreases the insulation quality of clothing and as sweat evaporates, your body cools. Adjust your clothing so that you do not sweat. Do this by partially opening your parka or jacket, by removing an inner layer of clothing, by removing heavy outer mittens or by throwing back your parka hood or changing to lighter headgear. The head and hands act as efficient heat dissipaters when overheated.

L: Wear your clothing loose and in layers

Wearing tight clothing and footgear restricts blood circulation and invites cold injury. It also decreases the volume of air trapped between the layers, reducing its insulating value. Several layers of lightweight clothing are better than one equally thick layer of clothing, because the layers have dead-air space between them. The dead-air space provides extra insulation. Also, layers of clothing allow you to take off or add clothing layers to prevent excessive sweating or to increase warmth.

D: Keep clothing dry

In cold temperatures, your inner layers of clothing can become wet from sweat and your outer layer, if not water repellent, can become wet from snow and frost melted by body heat. Wear water-repellent outer clothing, if available. It will shed most of the water collected from melting snow and frost. Before entering a heated shelter, brush off the snow and frost. Despite the precautions you take, there will be times when you cannot keep from getting wet. At such times, drying your clothing may become a major problem. You can place damp socks or mittens, unfolded, near your body so that your body heat can dry them. In a campsite, hang damp clothing inside the shelter near the top, using drying lines or improvised racks. You may even be able to dry each item by holding it before an open fire. Dry leather items slowly. If no other means are available for drying your boots, put them between your sleeping bag shell and liner. Your body heat will help to dry the leather.

A heavy, down-lined sleeping bag is a valuable piece of survival gear in cold weather. Ensure the down remains dry. If wet, it loses a lot of its insulation value. If you do not have a sleeping bag, you can make one out of parachute cloth or similar material and natural dry material, such as leaves, pine needles or moss. Place the dry material between two layers of the parachute material.

Top Cold-Weather Tools

Other important survival items are a knife; waterproof matches in a waterproof container, preferably one with a flint attached; a durable compass; map; watch; waterproof ground cloth and cover; flashlight; binoculars; dark glasses; fatty emergency foods; food gathering gear; and signaling items.

Remember, a cold weather environment can be very harsh. Give a good deal of thought to selecting the right equipment for survival in the cold. If unsure of an item you have never used, test it in an "overnight backyard" environment before venturing further. Once you have selected items that are essential for your survival, do not lose them after you enter a cold weather environment.

Information courtesy of the U.S. Army Survival Manual

Frostbite

If you're stuck in a cold-weather survival scenario, hypothermia is a threat. But there's also a little something called frostbite that could menace your fingers, toes, hands and feet. Frostbite is a cold-weather condition where your skin falls below the freezing point. This allows ice crystals to form within your skin cells, killing them in short order. If it sounds painful, that's because it is. You've probably experienced the tingling, numb feeling at some point in your life. This is a hint that frostbite is setting in.

Frostbite

Frostbite comes in two flavors -- superficial and severe. If you're able to re-warm your skin shortly after the initial freeze, you have the superficial variety and you'll recover. Severe frostbite is when the chill penetrates all the way to your muscles and bones. You'll notice some major tingling in your fingers and toes, and your skin's color and texture will change. If you're stricken with severe frostbite, you'll likely suffer tissue damage, which means that skin has actually died. If it's really severe, you may even need to have your fingers, toes, hands or feet amputated.

Stages of Frostbite

During the initial stages of frostbite, the skin turns red, then pasty white. After that, your skin hardens and blisters begin to form. From there, things get ugly. Your blisters will turn black and blue -- this is the most advanced stage of frostbite. If you're able to reverse the process by warming up soon enough, your skin may just fall off to reveal new skin growth underneath.

Warm Your Fingers and Toes

It's vital to rewarm your skin gradually. Cover your cold ears and warm your fingers under your armpits. Rubbing the damaged skin or submerging it in hot water will only cause more damage, so resist the temptation. Warm yourself with water between 100 and 106 degrees Fahrenheit (37.7 and 41 degrees Celsius). Get into a warmer area immediately, even if all you have available is a tent or shelter. Take off any tight clothing -- it restricts your blood flow. Your digits may have a tendency to stick together. You can avoid this by putting gauze or some kind of cloth between your fingers and toes to soak up excess moisture. Swelling is your enemy as well, so elevate the affected area to prevent this from happening. Get to a doctor as soon as you can if you have frostbite.

Dehydration

You've heard the phrase and probably even said it yourself -- "I'm dying of thirst." This common expression that means you're in need of a cool beverage becomes literal when you're faced with a survival scenario. Dehydration can kill you, which is why finding clean drinking water is at the top of the list when you're fighting for your life. Humans can only survive for a few days without water, and in hot, arid conditions, dehydration can set in within a few short hours.

Initial Stage

Dehydration goes far beyond thirst. Each and every cell and organ in your body needs water to function, so going without it for more than a few days can kill you. Hot conditions make matters worse because of water loss through perspiration, but we lose water in more ways than just sweat. You also lose it through your feces, urine and even your breath.

Progression

There are three stages of dehydration. During the first stage, you'll develop a serious case of "cotton mouth." You'll also pee less frequently, with decreased output, and your urine will have a deep color and strong odor. During the next stage, you'll urinate even less, your eyes will become dry and sunken, and your heart rate will increase. You know your dehydration is severe when you stop peeing completely, become lethargic and irritable, and you're overcome with nausea. Vomiting may also be in the cards, which will dehydrate you even more. If you fail to rehydrate once your situation becomes severe, you could fall into shock and die.

Hydration

Once you find some water, drink it slowly, but steadily. Drinking too fast may increase your nausea. Stay away from alcohol and caffeine -

- they'll just make you more dehydrated by increasing your urine output. If you're stranded on a desert island or stuck in a life raft in the ocean, stay away from the salt water. Drinking it will also cause you to become more dehydrated. You know you're in the clear when your nausea decreases, your energy increases, and your urine becomes clear and frequent. If you're going on an outdoor adventure, put some money into a good water filter before you go. This way any creek, river or lake can provide you with drinkable water.

Learn what foods to eat for survival in the wilderness.

(Warning, these foods may or may be editable by everyone)

Always know your allergies before attempting to eat wild foods!

Always know the plant before eating wild plants and animals.

Strongly suggest consulting a wild foods manual with details pictures and descriptions as well as consulting your doctor before obtaining and eating wild foods.

You're in the wilderness and a worse case scenario becomes a reality; you're lost. Let's make it even more harrowing: you have very little, or no, food.

What do you do?

Food is readily available in the wilderness areas if you know what to look for. Most of us have a hard time thinking about being hungry in the wild with no rescue in sight but if you take to any wilderness area these following tips will save your life.

First you should always have a small packable book detailing edible plants with you. This book should contain pictures of many plants that you can use for easily identifying plants and bulbs that will be edible and not poisonous. This small book should be available at any sporting goods store. In other words, how can you eat it with no way to identify it?

Never take a chance in the wilderness and eat a plant that you are not one hundred percent sure is edible. The effects of your decision can mean grave illness, hallucinations, kidney failure and even death if a mistake is made in this area. Always know what you are eating.

Depending on your activities, you can actually go without food for several weeks, although you should always remember to have adequate water for hydration available. You can die without water in as little as three days, but it takes some time to literally starve to death.

If you are short of drinking water limit the amount of food that you eat, and also limit it to as much sugars, starches and vegetation as possible. It takes three times the amount of water to digest proteins compared to starches and vegetation.

Gathering of edible plants allow you not only nutrition but many plants also carry substantial amounts of water. Be sure to gather all your greens in the morning before the sun comes out fully because the sun will strip these green plants of nutrients.

Some of these edible greens include Ferns, Clover, Dandelions, and almost all grasses that are seed bearing are edible.

The list of green edible plants is vast so consult your book if in doubt.

Many berries can be found at any elevation that are edible. Some of the edible berries are elderberry, cranberry, currants and gooseberry. Again I must suggest that you always consult your book and make sure that you are familiar with your choices in the wild because some of the berries are somewhat different in appearance. For instance, wild cranberries are much darker that commercial berries and do not grow in the traditional bogs.

DO NOT eat mushrooms. Why take the chance at all? Do Not eat any plant with milky sap unless you know for sure that it is edible. Some exceptions are wild figs and dandelions.

Teas can also be made easily from pine needles which are always available in any elevation. Look for Fir, Pine, and Spruce because these particularly contain high amounts of ascorbic acid which is an essential nutrient that will help prevent scurvy and other bone debilitating disease. Scurvy can happen quickly so always drink as much natural tea as possible.

Always remember, avoid shellfish, although sea urchin like starfish are edible anytime. Most shellfish have certain times of the year they are good, other times they emit toxins that can make them deadly. Starfish and other urchins can be split open and the insides and eggs should be removed and eaten.

All fur bearing animals are edible.

All birds are edible with no exceptions.

Grubs found in rotten logs are edible.

Snails can also be eaten once boiled sufficiently .

The inner bark of trees such as Poplar, Willows, Birches and Conifers are also edible as well as chock full of nutrients.

Learn how to identify and prepare edible wild plants. Also learn where to find them and if they have any nutritional value.

When picking edible plants it is crucial that you can properly identify them, because many are similar in appearance to poisonous plants. The optimum time to ensure proper identification is when the plants are flowering, since most have a unique appearance of flowers or fruits. To make extra certain if in doubt observe the plant through the growing season if it is possible.

BROOKLIME

This plant is found in the spring and summer in shallow water, swamps or ditches. It can be used in salad and as a potherb. The young shoots can be eaten before flowering, and the leaves can be eaten after flowering like watercress. Its leaves are oblong and toothed and there are one or two flowers in long simple clusters. The flowers may be lilac, rosy, bluish, or white in color. The fruit is a flattened and round capsule at the apex.

CAMASS BULBS

This plant is found in the mountain meadows and swamps of Washington, Oregon, and Northern California. It's flowers are usually blue. You can roast the bulbs by building a fire in a two foot deep pit. First place green wood over the fire. Then place some bark over the wood. Cover the bark with grass and leaves. Next put the bulbs over the bark. Finally, cover it with dirt or sand. The bulbs can also be prepared like potatoes.

CAT TAIL

Cat tail can be found in the spring and summer in or along side the fresh or brackish water of marshes and ponds. It can be used in salads, as a starchy vegetable,

bread, asparagus, cooked vegetable, soup, pickle, and jelly. It is a tall plant (up to 15 feet) with stiff pale-green leaves. The flower is a dense spike that changes in color from green to brown with a cotton-like material being produced on top as it grows. The young rootstocks have a sweet taste and are high in starchy material. They should be grated, boiled, and the starchy material drained out for use.

CHICKWEED

These annual plants can be used in salads and as potherbs. They are found in waste lots, gardens, and disturbed soils, and they survive winter frosts. It is good wholesome green vegetable that, when boiled, resembles spinach in taste. The leaves can also be eaten when boiled.

CLOVER

Clover can be used in salad, to make tea, as a breadstuff, and a potherb. The seeds and dried flowers can be used as a nutritious and wholesome bread food. It can be eaten raw or boiled. Eastern whites can be used to make clover tea by brewing the dried flower heads. It is best to dip clover leaves in salt water before eating or preparation to aid in digestion, and eating the leaves in excess can cause bloating.

COW PEA

These peas are found in thickets on roadsides and fields in the southern states and up into Indiana and Missouri. The look like any garden pea and they have great value as a food. They can be eaten green or after they've been dried.

DANDELION

This plant can be used as a potherb, in salad, and as a coffee substitute. Young leaves can be picked in early spring before the plant has flowered to add to salads, it can also be used in replace of spinach. The leaves should be boiled in two waters to rid bitterness. The roots can be ground to make a bitter coffee, and eaten for survival during a famine. Dandelion greens also have a tremendous amount of Vitamin A (25 times that of tomato juice and 50 times that of asparagus).

FOX GRAPES

They are mainly found in the south and Midwestern states, and are similar in appearance to Tokey grapes found in Californian fields. The grapes are very sour when eaten raw, but are good in jam or jelly without using Jell or pectin.

GINSENG

Ginseng is found in rich woods in the eastern US, but is nearly extinct in the wild. It can be used as food during a famine or emergency and for tea. It has a starchy quality when eaten raw, but is good when boiled in salty water. It's root is edible as well as aromatic. The leaves can be make into a good tea.

GREAT BURDOCK

Burdock is commonly found around abandoned buildings and manure piles and in residential yards in the northern US and in southern Canada. Peel the shoots and it can be eaten raw or with salad and vinegar. The stocks can be boiled or fried in butter. The peeled roots can be boiled in salt and pepper. Burdock can even be mashed into cakes and fried in butter.

INDIAN TURNIP

This plant has a peppery quality to it, and has long been used as a source of food in nature. It is not palatable when eaten raw. It should be thoroughly dried and then boiled or baked. To boil or roast it, dry it and then pound it into flour.

LAMB'S QUARTERS

Commonly regarded as a weed, this plant can be found in Europe and North America in damp or acidic soils from spring to fall. Lamb's quarters can be eaten as a

steamed vegetable or in soups and salads. In the summer it can be used as a potherb and in place of spinach.

MARSH MARIGOLDS

These are a marsh plant found in early spring in moist grounds and watery meadows, especially in clay or limestone areas. It has kidney-shaped green leaves with

orange-yellow flowers that resemble buttercups. The young leaves can be boiled to make greens, but make sure to boil for an hour or two and change the water at least once. It is

crucial that marsh marigolds are not eaten raw. They contain poisonous glucoside that is expelled during boiling.

MILK-WEED

Milk-weed is usually found from late spring and through summer in dry, open soil along roadsides, fences, and fields. It cab be used as a cooked vegetable, potherb, sugar, and to make chewing-gum. Young leaves can be washed and the prepared like spinach. The shoots can be prepared like asparagus after rubbing them in your hands to remove their wool. The seed-pods can be boiled and served with meat, or boiled in salted water, with a little soda, and then canned.

MUSTARD

Mustards are found in cultivated areas and in waste lands. When they are young they are popular as potherbs. To rid any bitterness the plant can be boiled in two waters.

Some mustard species' leaves can be used in salad. The seeds produce the powdered mustered used for seasoning. The roots can be pounded into pulp for meat garnish. Mustard also helps indigestion.

PERSIMMONS

Persimmons are a fruit that grows from trees that vary greatly in appearance, and grow wild in some states. They can be used to make jam, jelly, vinegar, beer, tea, a coffee substance and breadstuff. They should be gathered after the first frost when they are completely ripe and very soft. Persimmons can be eaten raw, seeds can be roasted and used for coffee, and dried fruits can be ground into meal to make bread. The fruit also can make a delicious syrup. To make the syrup, mix the persimmons with wheat bran, baked in pones. Put the mix in a container and pour water into it and let stand for 12 hours. Lastly, strain then boil to a thicker consistency.

PRICKLY PEAR

This plant bears delicious fruit in the south and can be found in sandy, dry and rocky soils. It looks like a cactus and the surface is covered with tufts of red brown tiny barbed bristles. The flowers are yellow with red centers. The parched seeds can be pulverized to make a soup thickening agent. The thick branches can be roasted in hot ashes and peeled to make a edible pulp.

ROSE FAMILY

Any plant from this family is edible. This includes blackberries, cloudberries, crab-apples, dewberries, raspberries, salmonberries, and thimbleberries. Many can be eaten raw and they also make good jams and jellies. They have green stems with dark green leaves They can grow upright and in trailing bushes. They usually flower and then produce sweet juicy fruit.

SQUAW ROOT

Squaw root is found in the Pacific states along the edges of woods and in meadows. The plant can grow up to four feet tall, with sparse small leaves and tiny white or pink flowers. It can be prepared by roasting, boiling, or baking.

THISTLES

Thistles have spiny tipped leaves and a red purple flower, and are found in fields across the United States. They can be used as potherb and in salads. Make sure to clip the spines off of the leaves before putting them in a salad. The roots can also be cooked and eaten too. A good way to prepare thistles is to first clip of the leaves, then peel off the shreds rind, cut up what's left and boil in salty water for five minutes or longer.

VIOLET

Violets have leaves and flowers that are edible and they can also be used to thicken soup. Young leaves can be used in salads, and the flowers can be used in jams. They can be used to thicken soups and may be added to wild okra and lamb's quarter.

WILD GARLIC

This plant can be easily recognized by it's potent and prevailing smell in rich meadows and alluvial woods in a variety of climatic conditions. It is used as a potherb, to treat wounds, to ease and prevent colds, and as a natural antibiotic. The bulbs are best tasting in the autumn or early spring, bulbettes are best in May or June, and young leaves used for seasoning are best picked in the early summer.

WILD RICE

Wild rice can be found in Minnesota, Wisconsin, Michigan, the Great Lakes area, and the upper Mississippian region. It is a broad-leaved grass that grows in water. It has broom like flower clusters with pollen carrying flowers on top and seed-bearing flowers on the bottom of the cluster. It must be harvested by boat. Once harvested it should be spread out and must be stirred as it sweats dry. Then put the rice over fire and stir, leaving the rice there until it is roasted. If you cannot roast it, put it in a place to dry and then thresh it. To thresh the rice you stomp on it with your feet.

WILD ONION

This plant is found in prairies, dry meadows, woodlands, and rocky slopes, and is easily identified by it's smell. It can also be recognized by it's white bell shaped flower atop a tree to four inch stem. Pick the onion before flowering, strip the outer coats, trim the

wilted leaves and then boil in salted water. The onion can also be used to season meats and other foods.

Testing Plants you Can Eat

Edibility of Plants

Plants are valuable sources of food because they are widely available, easily procured and, in the proper combinations, can meet all your nutritional needs.

WARNING: The critical factor in using plants for food is to avoid accidental poisoning. Eat only those plants you can positively identify and you know are safe to eat.

Absolutely identify plants before using them as food. Poison hemlock has killed people who mistook it for its relatives, wild carrots and wild parsnips.

At times you may find yourself in a situation for which you could not plan. In this instance you may not have had the chance to learn the plant life of the region in which you must survive. In this case you can use the Universal Edibility Test to determine which plants you can eat and those to avoid.

It is important to be able to recognize both cultivated and wild edible plants in a survival situation. Most of the information in this chapter is directed toward identifying wild plants because information relating to cultivated plants is more readily available. Remember the following when collecting wild plants for food:

* Plants growing near homes and occupied buildings or along roadsides may have been sprayed with pesticides. Wash them thoroughly. In more highly developed countries with many automobiles, avoid roadside plants, if possible, due to contamination from exhaust emissions.
* Plants growing in contaminated water or in water containing *Giardia lamblia* and other parasites are contaminated themselves. Boil or disinfect them.
* Some plants develop extremely dangerous fungal toxins. To lessen the chance of accidental poisoning, do not eat any fruit that is starting to spoil or

showing signs of mildew or fungus.

* Plants of the same species may differ in their toxic or sub toxic compounds content because of genetic or environmental factors. One example of this is the foliage of the common chokecherry. Some chokecherry plants have high concentrations of deadly cyanide compounds while others have low concentrations or none. Horses have died from eating wilted wild cherry leaves. Avoid any weed, leaves or seeds with an almond like scent, a characteristic of the cyanide compounds.

* Some people are more susceptible to gastric distress (from plants) than others. If you are sensitive in this way, avoid unknown wild plants. If you are extremely sensitive to poison ivy, avoid products from this family, including any parts from sumacs, mangoes and cashews.

* Some edible wild plants, such as acorns and water lily rhizomes, are bitter. These bitter substances, usually tannin compounds, make them unpalatable. Boiling them in several changes of water will usually remove these bitter properties.

* Many valuable wild plants have high concentrations of oxalate compounds, also known as oxalic acid. Oxalates produce a sharp burning sensation in your mouth and throat and damage the kidneys. Baking, roasting or drying usually destroys these oxalate crystals. The corm (bulb) of the jack-in-the-pulpit is known as the "Indian turnip," but you can eat it only after removing these crystals by slow baking or by drying.

WARNING: Do not eat mushrooms in a survival situation! The only way to tell if a mushroom is edible is by positive identification. There is no room for experimentation. Symptoms of the most dangerous mushrooms affecting the central nervous system may show up after several days have passed when it is too late to reverse their effects.

Other Plants That Can Be Eaten

Recommedation to purchase a pocket plant identifier to ensure that the plant is identified correctly prior to eating.

* Arrowroot (*Sagittaria* species)
* Asparagus (*Asparagus officinalis*)
* Beechnut (*Fagus* species)
* Blackberries (*Rubus* species)
* Blueberries (*Vaccinium* species)
* Burdock (*Arctium lappa*)
* Cattail (*Typha* species)
* Chestnut (*Castanea* species)
* Chicory (*Cichorium intybus*)
* Chufa (*Cyperus esculentus*)
* Dandelion (*Taraxacum officinale*)
* Daylily (*Hemerocallis fulva*)
* Nettle (*Urtica* species)
* Oaks (*Quercus* species)
* Persimmon (*Diospyros virginiana*)
* Plantain (*Plantago* species)
* Pokeweed (*Phytolacca americana*)
* Prickly pear cactus (*Opuntia* species)
* Purslane (*Portulaca oleracea*)
* Sassafras (*Sassafras albi um*)
* Sheep sorrel (*Rumex acetosella*)
* Strawberries (*Fragaria* species)
* Thistle (*Cirsium* species)
* Water lily and lotus (*Nuphar, Nelumbo* and other species)
* Wild onion and garlic (*Allium* species)
* Wild rose (*Rosa* species)
* Wood sorrel (*Oxalis* species)

TROPICAL AREA FOOD PLANTS

* Bananas (*Musa* species)
* Breadfruit (*Artocarpus incisa*)
* Cashew nut (*Anacarium occidental*)
* Coconut (*Cocos nucifera*)
* Mango (*Mangifera indica*)
* Palms (various species)
* Papaya (*Carica* species)
* Sugarcane (*Saccharum officinarum*)
* Taro (*Colocasia* species)

DESERT AREA FOOD PLANTS

* Acacia (*Acacia farnesiana*)
* Agave (*Agave* species)
* Cactus (various species)
* Date palm (*Phoenix actylifera*)
* Desert amaranth (*Amaranths palmeri*)

SEAWEEDS

One plant you should never overlook is seaweed. It is a form of marine algae found on or near ocean shores. There are also some edible freshwater varieties. Seaweed is a valuable source of iodine, other minerals and vitamin C. Large quantities of seaweed in an unaccustomed stomach can produce a severe laxative effect.

When gathering seaweeds for food, find living plants attached to rocks or floating free. Seaweed washed onshore any length of time may be spoiled or decayed. You can dry freshly harvested seaweeds for later use.

Its preparation for eating depends on the type of seaweed. You can dry thin and tender varieties in the sun or over a fire until crisp. Crush and add these to soups or broths. Boil thick, leathery seaweeds for a short time to soften them. Eat them as a vegetable or with other foods. You can eat some varieties raw after testing for edibility.

- **Seaweeds**

* Dulse (*Rhodymenia palmata*)
* Green seaweed (*Ulva lactuca*)
* Irish moss (*Chondrus crispus*)
* Kelp (*Alaria esculenta*)
* Laver (*Porphyra* species)
* Mojaban (*Sargassum fulvellum*)
* Sugar wrack (*Laminaria saccharina*)

Food Bourne Illness

Anyone who has ever gotten a touch of food poisoning will tell you that spending the night hugging the toilet isn't a pleasant experience. Now imagine not having the relief that comes with a supply of fresh drinking water to rehydrate you or a comfy bed to regain your strength. Picture yourself alone and lost in the woods with no shelter. This is what's known as a worst-case scenario. Food-borne illness can leave you weak and unable to function. If you're stuck in a survival scenario, it can even kill you.

Sour Stomach

If you have some survival skills and you're able to hunt down or trap an animal for food, make sure you cook it all the way through and then some. There's no such thing as medium rare in this situation. Eating tainted or undercooked meat can mean you're chowing down on some serious bacteria like E. coli or salmonella -- not ideal when you're struggling to survive. You can also become ill by eating the wrong plant or insect.

Both Ends

Any kind of food-borne bacteria will lead to some serious diarrhea, nausea and vomiting. If things get worse, you might feel some abdominal cramping and fever setting in. In a survival scenario, food-borne disease becomes especially dangerous because you're losing fluids every time you pass food from either end, which leads to dehydration and weakness.

What to Avoid

It may be tempting, but even the freshest road kill is something you should avoid at all costs. It doesn't matter if it's a potential meal; it could already be swimming with harmful bacteria. If you have no meat options and you're relying on insects and plants to provide your nourishment, avoid anything that's brightly colored, extremely pungent or has thorns or spikes. That's nature's way of saying, "don't eat me." Plants with a milky sap are also a no-no.

Insects

If insects are on the menu, pull off the legs, arms and head, and cook the body by boiling or roasting it for the best taste. You can eat most edible insects raw, but a nice rack of grasshopper skewers is sure to bring a smile to a survivalist's face. The legs and head won't offer much protein anyway, and it can help the flavour to get rid of them.

Waterborne Illness

The first thing on your priority list in any kind of worst-case survival scenario is a drinkable water source. Ideally, this means some kind of natural running water -- a stream, river or spring. If that's not possible, you'll need to collect your own water using some basic survival techniques. A lack of food resources may leave you hungry and fatigued, but not having water will kill you in just a few days. What can really put a dent in your bid to survive is drinking contaminated water. Failing to purify what you find or collect could make you very sick, weak and unable to function -- not good if you want to live through your worst-case scenario.

It's in the Water

The Center for Disease Control and Prevention says that nearly 1 billion people worldwide don't have access to safe, clean drinking water. Mainly these are people living in developing countries. But no matter where you are, if you're travelling off the beaten path and find yourself lost or stranded, you could have a hard time finding clean water. There's a host of things in tainted water that can make you sick. Parasites, bacteria, viruses and protozoa can be found in water all over the world, and you don't want them swimming around in your stomach.

Run Water, Run

Running water is your best bet and can often be consumed without even purifying it. But it's typically a good idea to go with a "better safe than sorry" approach, even with running water, which means boiling whatever you find for 10 minutes. This will kill any bacteria or virus and give you some safe, drinkable water, not to mention peace of mind. If you're staring death in the face from dehydration and don't have the means to boil water, go ahead and drink unpurified running water. Standing water should be an absolute last resort.

Be Prepared!

If you know you'll be roughing it or going on an exotic adventure, be smart and take along some items that you could need in case of an emergency. You can buy a compact emergency water filter that's no bigger than a large drinking straw and stash it in your backpack. You can also pick up some purification tablets for emergency use. These tablets use iodine or chlorine to treat water and make it safe for consumption.

Plant Rashes and Irritations

Plants can be your best friend or worst enemy in a survival scenario. They can be a source of food and water, provide shade and shelter, or even come in handy as rudimentary clothing -- just ask Adam and Eve about their fig leaves. But eating the wrong plant can make you very sick, and even touching one can leave you with some gnarly skin issues. You won't die from touching the wrong plant, but a serious case of poison ivy without the relief of a remedy can hamper your chances of success in a survival scenario. And scratching the itch can lead to infection and bigger problems.

Itchy and Scratchy

Poison ivy, oak and sumac are the three most likely culprits in the wild. In the United States, especially in the mountains of the East and Pacific Northwest, these three green plants are found everywhere you turn. The old rule of thumb is easy to remember and will save you every time -- "leaves three, leave it be." If you see bright green leaves in groups of three, there's a good chance it will be either poison ivy or oak. Sumac shrubs and trees, which are 5 to 20 feet (1.5 to 6 meters) tall, have seven to 14 leaves per stem.

Other Itchy Plants

While ivy, oak and sumac are the most plentiful plants that can cause dermatitis, or skin irritation, you should also be on the lookout for boxwood leaves, century plants, ginkgo seeds, horse apple sap, oleander leaves, pawpaw fruit and trumpet creeper leaves. Do yourself a favor and either grab a book on the local flora or do some Internet research so you can identify offending plants when you travel.

Rash Decisions

If you mess up and you're suddenly covered in an annoying, itchy rash, fight the temptation to scratch for relief. Not only will this help spread the rash, but you could also develop an infection. If you know you've come into contact with one of these plants, wash the area that you touched immediately with soap and water, and you may be able to avoid the rash setting in. Make sure your first aid kit is stocked with some skin helpers. Calamine lotion and hydrocortisone cream are good to have on hand. They won't cure the rash, but they'll aid in the itch factor. Applying cool compresses or running cold river water over the rash may also help to thwart the itch

Heat Stroke

Maybe you're an adventure traveler trekking the Sahara on foot. Perhaps an ocean storm has left you shipwrecked on a deserted island in the middle of the summer. Or maybe you're just overexerting yourself with yard work and ignoring the signs to slow down and cool off. There are plenty of scenarios where you might suffer from heatstroke.

Feel the Heat

When you overheat, your body is failing to regulate its core temperature because of a dramatic loss of salt and water through excessive sweating. Every cell in your body needs water to perform, and the sodium and chlorine in salt keep your muscles functioning properly. If you overheat, you'll get heat cramps, followed by heat exhaustion and, finally, heatstroke.

The Stroke

When you fall victim to heatstroke, your body has completely failed to regulate its temperature, and you can no longer sweat to cool down. You'll know you're in the midst of

heatstroke if you experience severe headaches, dizziness, nausea and vomiting, muscle twitches or spasms, confusion and aggression, red or hot skin, an increased heart rate, hallucinations or unconsciousness.

Cooling Down

f you experience symptoms of heatstroke, head for some shade and lie down. Elevate your feet, loosen your clothing and drink water. If you're with someone else, pour cool water on your skin and have them fan you vigorously. If you're alone, fan yourself without expending too much energy. Even in a survival scenario when water is scarce, don't conserve your H2O -- heatstroke can kill you. Douse a towel, shirt or bandana in some cool water and apply it to your armpits and groin area to help lower your overall body temperature.

Recovery

Once you start to cool down, you need to lie flat in the shade for a while. A good way to tell if your condition is improving is if your nausea subsides and your heart rate chills out to a steady, normal level. Once these things happen, you can think about moving again. When you do attempt to get up and walk around, take it nice and slow and continue to drink water. Stay in the shade as much as you can for the rest of your day. If you're at home, take the rest of the day off from yard work -- the grass can wait.

Bug Bites and Stings

Bugs. There aren't many things on the planet that can hamper outdoor fun like flies, mosquitoes, bees and ticks. Getting bitten or stung can ruin a picnic or pleasant patio time in a flash. But in a worst-case survival scenario, these bites and stings can put you in danger. If you're allergic to bee stings and you're caught without your remedy, you can even die. Ticks and mosquitoes spread diseases like malaria, yellow and dengue fevers, and Lyme disease. In fact, mosquito-borne disease kills more people around the world than anything else. When you add the spiders and scorpions that live in the wild, it becomes clear that size doesn't matter in a survival scenario.

Ticks

It's important to give your body and scalp a good once-over a couple of times a day and before you go to sleep. If you locate a tick, and it's burrowed into your skin, cut off its air supply by covering it with Vaseline or tree sap. You can also burn it with a hot match or ember, causing it to release its hold. Use tweezers if you have them; make sure you remove the entire tick and immediately wash the area with soap and water.

Bees

If you're nailed by a bee or wasp, get the stinger and venom sac out as quickly as you can by scraping it with a clean knife blade. Then wash the area thoroughly with soap and water. If you have a cigarette, open it up and put some wet tobacco on the sting to help neutralize the pain.

Mosquito

Buzzing mosquitoes are more than annoying -- they can be deadly. If you know you're traveling to a jungle area, get immunized against malaria and any other mosquito-spread diseases before you go, and take along some DEET insect repellent for good measure. When you get bitten by the mosquito -- and it will happen -- try not to scratch the area to avoid infection. A good trick to reduce the itch: cover the bite with some mud and let it dry.

Spiders

Venomous spider bites may not hurt much initially, but local pain will develop and then spread over your entire body. You'll likely encounter stomach cramps, nausea and vomiting, weakness, tremors and sweating. If you're bitten, clean the area immediately and try to identify the culprit. Or even better, capture the spider for identification. Knowing what kind of venom you have in your blood can help save your life.

How To Build A Live Animal Trap

A live animal trap can be used to trap injured animals, control rodent populations or to catch the runaway family pet. Whatever the reason, you can easily build an effective live animal trap yourself. These instructions will help you build a box trap that will catch almost any kind of live animal you want, depending on the size of the box you choose to make.

Step 1: Beginning the Box

Attach two of the 1x2-inch pieces of wood on the edge of one of the 2x2-foot pieces of plywood. Attach with wood glue first, then secure with the nails or screws. Attach another 1x2 directly across from it on the other side of the 2x2. Do this to three pieces of the plywood.

Step 2: Reinforce the Box

Start to form a box shape with four pieces of plywood. Two pieces with the reinforced edged should be opposite of each other as well as two un-reinforced opposite each other use the wood glue and screws or nails to form a box with an open top and bottom. Screw or nail the last piece of reinforced plywood to the top. Do not forget to use the glue first. You can use additional pieces of 1 x 2 wood to reinforce the box if it is weak in any areas. Some places that might need reinforcement are the inside corners of the box.

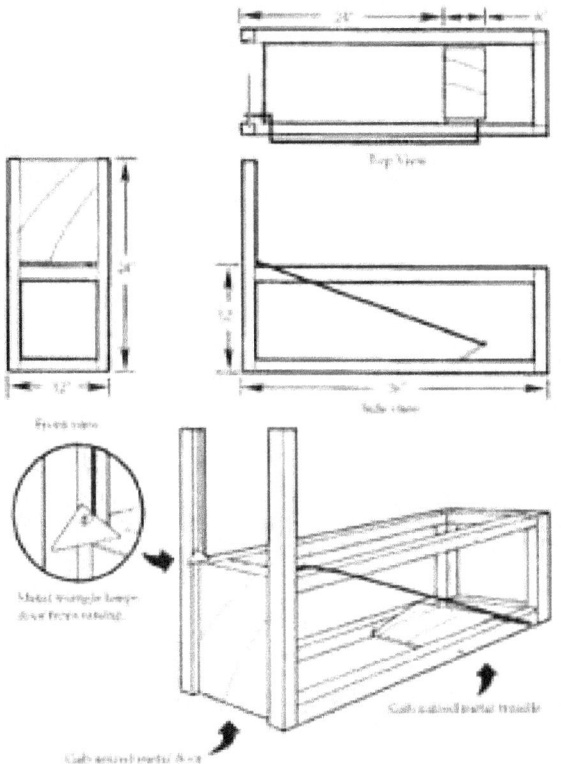

Step 3: Set your Bait and Trap

Now that you have a heavy duty box it is time to set the bait and trap. Place the box in the area where you are most likely to catch what you are after. You will use the piece of PVC to prop one end of the box up for your animal to enter. Attach the bait you choose to one end of the wire. The wire is going to act as the bait and the trigger. Place about two inches of the wire into the box directly between the PVC and the box. The bait side should be inside the box.

Step 4: Wait For Your Animal

When the animal enters the box it will start to tug at the bait. The trigger will respond by wiggling loose from the PVC and shutting the box with the animal inside. Check your trap daily to make sure that if you do catch something that you are able to transfer it as soon as possible. You also want to make sure that nothing gets trapped unintentionally.

You can also use pre-made boxes that can hold the animal that you are trying to catch. One thing that you might also want to do is drill some air holes into the box, we all like fresh air. Whatever your reason for needing to catch a live animal these few steps will have you well on your way.

Simple ways to trap animals.

To trap animals, or trapping, is a skill that takes practice, like any other survival skill. If you are a beginner to trapping, use the information here as a starter.

* The primitive trapping techniques described here are only for wilderness survival situations. Obey the rules and trapping regulations of the area you are visiting. *

As a trapper, you can set many traps and snares, all working for you simultaneously and for 24 h every day. Regular checking of traps is crucial to minimize any suffering to the animal. Go for small prey, especially birds. All birds are edible, but some taste better than others.

Trails

The presence of wild animals can often be determined by their tracks in the snow, sand or soft mud. These trails are excellent places to set snares or traps. Following these trails in your search for prey will often lead to water-holes and feeding places. Animal Tracks and tracking in general, is fascinating.

Prey

You must determine what you are trying to catch and set your traps, specifically with those animals in mind. Look for any natural bottleneck along the track where you may use your traps or snares. Position your traps and snares where that animal passes through.

Avoid disturbing the area as much as possible. Don't alarm the prey by leaving signs of your presence. Animals avoid humans and are very suspicious, hide your scent. If possible wear gloves when you handle the trap or hold the snaring material over smoke or underwater for a few minutes.

How To Build A Deadfall Trap (and Survive in the Wild)

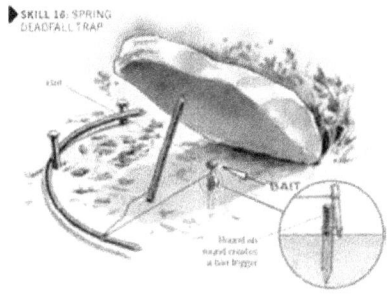

A simple and effective way to trap animals is to use the dead fall trap.

Locate the animal trail and burrow if possible to determine where to place your deadfall trap. You may have to observe the creature for several days along its hunting or foraging route to find the best spot.

Find a large flat rock with a weight significantly heavy enough to crush or pin a small animal, and locate 3 fine or thin twigs of 3 different lengths proportionate to the size and weight of the rock. You should have 1 long twig, 1 twig of half the size of the longer one and 1 twig long enough to place sufficiently under the rock horizontally.

Cut a niche in one of the shorter twigs a few inches from one end, and set it aside. In another longer twig, cut another niche in the center, and stand the rock up with the longer twig. Place another medium size twig horizontally or perpendicular to your vertical twig on the niche leading under the rock.

Brace the perpendicular twigs with the smaller twig on top at a 45-degree angle. You will need to set this up, and mark your horizontal twig to cut another niche so the smaller twig locks into place

Place bait on the horizontal twig at the end underneath the rock, and place bait along the trail leading up to the deadfall trap consisting of the animal's favorite foods. You may have to observe or research the diet of the animal you wish to trap to ensure positive results.

Snare trap

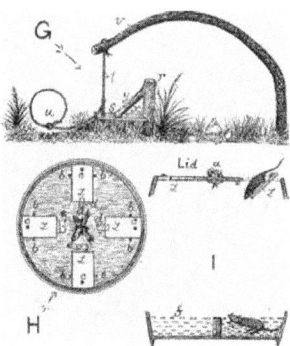

Use snares to trap small animals is a simple method. Snare wire should be part of your survival kit if not, you can improvise with ropes, strings, fishing lines, or shoelaces.

Make sure the noose is large enough to pass freely over the animal's head. Set it at a height that's equal to the height of the animals head and a hand's width from an obstruction. Support it with small branches to make sure the noose is in the appropriate position. Then anchor securely.

www.ingramcontent.com/pod-product-compliance
Lightning Source LLC
Chambersburg PA
CBHW070610290526
45790CB00002B/851